AWAKE

TIME TO FIND YOUR WAY BACK HOME

Isabella Maria Rösli

Isabella Maria Rösli
© 2024 Isabella Maria Rösli
Cover Design & Illustration: Isabella Maria
Rösli Editing: Patrick Anderson
Pages - 255
ISBN: 978-3-7597-2220-1
Print: BoD . Books on Demand GmbH,
In de Tarpen 42, 22848 Norderstedt
Publish: Libri Plureos GmbH, Friedensallee
273, 22763 Hamburg

To all the beautiful souls
who taught me lessons about love.

To all the beautiful souls
who saw me when I didn't see myself.

To all the beautiful souls
who were angels and teachers
in my path through life.

Hey, my love, my wonderful soul

This book is for you,
I want to share all the thoughts that helped me
to heal and reconnect with my true self.

This book wants to inspire you
and is here for your awakening.

We will go through my way of falling into the
deepest pain and finding my way back
to the purest feeling of bliss.

May it remind you to be kind to yourself
and let you realize that you are nothing that
needs to be fought.

May it help you to find the healing you are
searching for.

May it release pressure and let you find your way
back to pure love.

May it let you realize who you really are.

Honey, let's start,
my wish is that on every page of this book,
you find back to your heart
and that it opens a new world for you.

All my love for you.

Isabella Maria

CHAPTERS IN THIS BOOK

1

CHAPTER

to fall down

Wherever you are in life right now,
there's a reason why you need to be
exactly there.

You are exactly where
you are supposed to be

ALWAYS

The moment will come when you will
understand why this happened to you.

It will make sense, trust it.

Pain is part of life,
but suffering because of that pain
is always a choice.

You are not only this pain.
You are so much more than that.

I know life is really hard sometimes,
maybe you want to give up
but never forget
you are here right now,
you came so far,
don't give up, just because
it's not easy right now.

You can do that and deep in yourself
you know that you were born
to be a warrior of life,
so keep moving on.

As children, we fall down
again and again.

But we also get up again
until we learn to stand
on our feet.

That's exactly how it is in life:
we will always fall down, fail,
and make mistakes, but each of
these experiences makes us
stronger and wiser.

Life lets you fall because it
knows that you are strong
enough to get back up
and keep going.

Every tear you cry
will nourish the flowers
that will bloom
inside of you.

Never ever be ashamed
of who you are, my love.

What you should never forget:
You don't have
to fight against yourself.
You don't have
to be hard on yourself and
hate yourself.
You can always choose
who you want to be and
how you want to treat yourself.

Choose to be someone
who *definitely* deserves love.

You live in a society that wants
to make you feel not enough
all the time.

Don't believe it, not even once.

You are enough
and you will always be enough.

Some days it felt
like my anxiety was eating me up
from the inside,
and I tried everything
to run away from it.

Until I realized
that resistance is useless
and that we will never find peace
in resisting
but in *accepting what is*.

You are destined for greatness,
never forget that.

You don't have to be addicted to pain
or fighting against yourself
just to feel alive.

You are like a phoenix.
Sometimes you have to burn.
Something in you has to
crumble to ashes,
so that something new
can arise in you.

Sometimes storms surround you,
sometimes they rage inside you,
but always know
that you are not the storm

you are the holy lighthouse
that will always be firmly anchored
in the ground
and will never ever stop shining.

Sometimes your light will be dim,
but it will never be gone.
Because it is what you are.

And in the storm
never forget
you don't need to fight

just surrender

and silence will guide you to peace.

Some facts about the pain you feel:

It's only a feeling.
Just like it comes, so it will go.

Pain is like a crying baby,
it only wants to be seen,
wants some words of love,
and wants to feel welcome.

You can't press it away,
because there is a reason
why it is there.

Your evaluation of it
decides what you will become
out of it.

It is not the pain that hurts,
but your fear and resistance to it.

Pain strives for healing,
that's why you feel it.

Why are you ashamed of yourself
any longer?

Do you think it's worth it
to keep opening up the wounds of
your past?

You deserve to let go.

Yes, it happened to you.
But it is the past and
you can't change what happened.

You can only change
what you make out of it.

How long are you willing to keep
fighting against yourself,
even though the battle was already
lost a long time ago?

And even when the sun goes down
it doesn't mean that there
will never be light again.

Life only whispers:
"Now you are ready for the darkness.
You are ready to realize
that you don't need light on the outside
just to be able to shine by yourself"

I wish I could show you
how valuable you are
and the greatest pain
I will forever feel
is to let go of that desire
and let you discover your worth
by yourself.

But I will always be there and do my
best to *walk this path by your side*.

In the biggest pain,
to grow to the stars

Blaming others for your feelings,
my dear,
will never bring you the liberation
you desire.

True freedom comes
when you fall in peace
with how others have treated you.

That doesn't mean it was okay,
but that you don't let others decide
who you are.

Your past does not define
who you are.
Yes, it is part of your history.
But you decide who you have
become through your past.

Time for a new chapter...

You don't need to define your
existence by the things
you need to become.

*Maybe life is more about being
than becoming.*

Life breaks you in many parts
so that you can put yourself
back together and see
who you really are.

Sometimes life will overwhelm you.
And that is absolutely valid.
Life is not like a piece of furniture.
You have not been given an
instruction sheet for
your life here on earth.

The only thing you know is
that you exist here.
Let that be reason enough
to celebrate yourself every single day.

Yes, it may not be easy,
but you are still here.

You are an incredibly brave soul and
the hero of your own life.

You are not the victim
of your circumstances.
You are so much more.
You make yourself a victim,
that's the difference.

If you knew what you really are,
you would be lost for words,
it would amaze you.

Never ever make yourself
smaller than you are.

Maybe you would give everything
to finally be able to control your life.

But striving to control your life
will always be for nothing.

My love, you cannot control your life,
it is an illusion.
I know it may hurt, but that's the truth.

But you can decide who you are and how
you respond to the experiences life
brings you.
Not knowing what life will bring you
is also the greatest adventure.

I know uncertainty scares us,
maybe we can learn to make peace
with the fear of that
and remember that life
always wants the best for us.

Trust, let go, and be at peace
with whatever life brings you.
Everything is and will be okay.

You are sometimes afraid
like all people.
It's okay.
Fear makes you human
and that is why you are here.

Never forget that fear
only wants to protect you,
it is not your enemy
so stay kind to your fear,
make fear your friend,
and walk *hand in hand* with it.

Feeling your fear doesn't make you
weak, it makes you *incredibly strong*.

Some days feel like
being floated around in the deepest
and darkest parts of the ocean

hopeless, numb, like sleeping, sad,
lonely, and full of fear.

But there are also days that feel like
the brightest, filled with pure magic,
love and joy

Who am I to decide that one
of them is better?

No, it's just living life
in *its deepest expression.*

Feeling empty doesn't mean that something inside you is broken, it means that *something new* wants to grow inside of you.

Your darkness is not your enemy
it is just the trigger you need
to bring your *inner alchemist* to life.

You can transform everything,
heal yourself
and you can dance the dance between
darkness and light.

This is life.

As the moon shines in the sky,
the sun will rise again in the morning.

Don't hold on to anything
because everything is a phase.

Don't be afraid
that it will never be different again,
everything is in constant change,
so *trust that the sun will rise again.*

Give life *a chance* to express itself
through you.

You are here to live
and not to stand still.

Falling down is your destiny.

Life doesn't want you to suffer,
it wants you to become stronger and
to let you remember who you really are.

With each fall, life wants to give you
the opportunity to learn.

Life is telling you:
*"I know you are strong enough
to learn something and get up again".*

You are allowed to feel anger
and *still be lovable*.

Every moment of pain
is an *opportunity* for healing.

Sometimes I am so afraid of being alone that I *feel alon*e.

It is not your feelings that are hard,
but the resistance to your feelings
that makes it hard.

Your job is not to swim in your feelings,
but to *surf on them*.

Maybe you have given up
like we all do sometimes.

But never forget,
the *warrior inside of you*
will never fall asleep

and will always fight
for your life.

2

CHAPTER

surrender

The true path to freedom lies
in letting go of how it should be

and *accepting it*
as it is.

Acceptance of what is
create space
to *simply be.*

It is not your job to be only love.
Your task is to be human,
in *all its facets*.

In fear, in sadness, in anger, in pain and
in the acceptance of your vulnerability.

Dare to feel real,
stop running away from yourself
and open up to life again.

You were born into a world where you
were told from the beginning
what you could and could not be.
You were taught that it is not enough
to be what you are.

That you are too much,
that you are too little,
that you have to do things to earn love.

The truth is:
That *you are welcome* just as you are.

You were born into a world
where you can be anything
and there is room for everything.

Since the moment of your birth,
this world has become
so much more beautiful.

You enrich this world
and your uniqueness is needed.

You are here as you are
because *you are on a mission,*
it's about touching hearts,
making "mistakes",
falling down and standing up again,
learning as much as you can,
creating change,
finding healing and
enriching this world with *your uniqueness.*

It doesn't matter what people
have told you what you are,
you don't have to be anything else
than yourself.

What really sets you free
is the ability to let go.

Letting go is not a loss,
it is what you have to do,
and it is the price you pay
to be free.

I know it's not easy,
but you can learn how to do it.

Let go and become free.

Honey.
Sometimes it *just takes time*
Stay patient.
The time will come.

Sometimes there is just this
deep sadness and you don't know
where it comes from.
You don't always have to understand.
Just be with it.

Healing begins when we stop fighting
and resisting.

We don't need to understand
everything
to be able to find healing.

Surrender and be with it.

You can fight it or you can accept it.

With the first option,
you will never be able to find peace.
It is like a war.
The war will never be ended by
another war,
but by the *end of the war*.

Fighting or resisting
creates a stronger attack back.

Letting go and accepting
creates peace.

Every person is broken, but that doesn't
mean that you are destroyed.
Brokenness means being human.

We are all here
to put our inner broken parts
back together
and get a bigger picture
of our unique existence
here in this world.

Maybe you think you're weird or don't
fit into this society the way you are.

What if,
the reason why you feel that way
is because you are here to create a new
world where everything has a place?

Where you don't have to be anything
else than yourself.

Maybe you are not weird at all, but you
think you are, because here, everybody
plays a role and *you are just real...*

The moment you will become free
is the moment you let go
of the need for acknowledgment
from others.

This is the *highest form of living*
and the highest form of healing
in this life.

You can stop searching or
copying others
because you think
you have to be something else.

All that needs to be found
is yourself.

It's time to find your *way back home*.

If you were never sad, you wouldn't
know what it feels like to be happy.

It's okay to be lost sometimes
but just because you feel that way
doesn't mean that you are lost.

You are *exactly where you need to be,*
remember that.

I know maybe you hate yourself.
You hate yourself
not because of who you are,
but because others have told you
that you are not enough
the way you are.

You direct the rejection and hate on
the outside against yourself.

You continue with
what others have started.
Please, my love, *it's time to stop that.*

She began to take the storm by the hand.
And they *dance through life* together.

There is a *whole universe* inside you,
and you decide what it looks like.

Finding yourself means that
wherever you are in the world,
home is always there
because *home is what you are.*

Your story doesn't have to be
finished just to bring it to life.
Go into the unknown,
let yourself be guided
and the *story will be written by itself.*

You don't find out who you are
if you try to be anything else
than yourself all the time.

You, yourself
are the guide you are looking for.

Life is tough enough
why do we throw stones
in our own way?

and fill our minds with hate
our thoughts with shame?

when will it be enough?

when will we stop only existing
as we should be and surrender
to the rare being we are?

because there is a place for you
and this place, yeah that's you.

Feeling lonely and being lonely
are not the same thing.

You are *never alone*, even if it seems so.

You do not have to be perfect
to call yourself spiritual.

We all act
as if we have found
all the answers.

but we are all seekers
seemingly lost in *endless possibilities*.

At some point, there came a time
when I gave up being something
because I just wanted to be.

Let your life be a path
that is *moved by grace.*

For yourself.
For others.
And for your life.

Sometimes I feel like the loneliest
person in the whole world.

I would love to get into a rocket and
land on a planet all by myself,
get away from all the pain, suffering,
misunderstandings and problems.

But then there are days when I could
wish for nothing else than to embrace
every human being on this earth and
give away all my love.

Maybe my heart will always be a bit
lonely and I know that one day
I will find peace with it.

Every one of us
lost trust in each other.
So don't blame yourself
for just needing time to heal
and find your way back
to the knowledge
that we're all the same
and not different.

Maybe the things
that are happening in the world
are touching you as much
as they touch me,
maybe you are just disappointed
by all the pain you see
because you know we could all do better.

I know it's not easy
but be the solution
to the pain you see on the outside

"Just *be the answer*."

Life is not about being the best,
life is about being yourself.
And *this is the best*.
For you.
And for us all.

I know you are searching for meaning,
for yourself and for inner peace.

Maybe the salvation we are looking for
is not finding the answers,
but giving up the search.

Maybe we don't have to find anything
but instead
surrender to life,

knowing that we don't have
to understand
in order to be alive.

Perhaps our healing comes not
from fighting pain
or forcing ourselves to be perfect,
but from surrender to our darkness
and acknowledging our humanity.

Because you are here,
this world is so much more beautiful.

I always searched for the one medicine
that would heal my soul
but maybe it's not one thing,
but *life at all*.

We can let go of the pressure
of becoming perfect through healing
and let go of the need to do something
to become whole.

Life will send us the right persons,
wisdom, the right situations
that will teach us
how to bring ourselves home.

And in that moment I found peace
not because I was still trying to become,
instead I realized life is *here to be*.

Be brave enough to grow your roots
down deep
to land on this earth
and find your place
in a world that wants you different
than you might be.

It is your birthright to be here
exactly as you are.

Your place is here

You always give your best – *be kind*.

Don't forget:
When you feel lost in your life,
you aren't lost, you *just feel like that*.

It's okay to also be with that phase,
just as it comes, so it will go.

You are always where you need to be
and you're never alone.

Every one of us
wants to get better and better.
We always see what
doesn't exist right now,
and we get frustrated by it.

But my love, do not forget
how far you have come.

Your roots are deeper
than you think,
the little seed you were years ago
becomes the strong tree
you grow into it.

3

CHAPTER

find healing

Maybe life
is not about achieving happiness,
but being able to be *with everything*.

Passion over Pressure.
You have time.
Do what makes you smile.
Let go of what you think you need to do
and go *your own unique path*.

Loneliness,
the worst feeling I've ever felt

the lies I began to tell myself
about the love I didn't deserve

that I am too weird
too crazy
too much for the world

but one day I realized,
that the loneliness I feel every day,

doesn't make me weird,
it makes me a human being
and lets me be a part of others,

because loneliness is the feeling
every one of us feels.

Your body may not look the way others
told you it should look.
It may have scars,
it may not be "perfectly" formed,
your skin may not be flawless,
you may have hair on your body,
wrinkles on your face,
you may not fit
into the common ideal of beauty.
Doesn't that just mean that you are alive?
that you are just real?

Look, people have made you feel
like you have to look a certain way
to deserve love,
but who has the right to tell you
how you have to look to be enough?
Your body is just right the way it is.

It's not about what it looks like,
it's about what it allows you to do.

Butterflies are not born with wings,
first they crawl on the ground.
This is their *journey of life*.

Just because the wings
need to be developed
doesn't mean they
weren't *born with them*.

The world tries
to make you gray.

But never forget
that you carry a whole rainbow of colors
in yourself.

The world needs *your colors*,
don't hide them, even for a second.

About the pain in the world:
All the pain, injustice, war and abuse
that exists in this world hurts you,
I understand that.

Because you are this world.

You can change this world,
never doubt it.
You have hope in you, never lose it.

*Because there is always hope
and you are the proof of it.*

Don't be afraid to move the world
with your differences
to let the masks fall
to stand by your uniqueness
and to realize someday
that through your courage
and vulnerability
you could remind others
that they are all allowed to stand
in their authenticity too.

We became good
at looking away from our pain,
hiding wounds with band-aids,
pretending we are not
deeply shaken and hurt.

We think healing happens when we
pretend pain does not exist,

but healing happens when
we are brave enough to look
into the depth of our vulnerability.

It is easy to hate something
that is hated by others.
But it is not easy to love something
that has been hated by others.

Choose truly.

healing takes:
a clear decision
time
the honesty and courage to feel deeply
patience
a lot of compassion for you
the ability to forgive (yourself and others)
the courage to let go
and the will not to give up

Why is life so hard, I ask myself?

"Life is not hard.
All you are here for
is to surrender to me
and trust me again.
Everything is good".
Answers life.

You have become blind to what you are,
because *you only see what is not there.*

What is the meaning of life?

For me, the *meaning of life*
is life itself.
All the facets that your life offers you,
all the opportunities to learn,
find out what love is about,
all the moments in which life
brings you everything to heal and
guide your way back home to yourself.

Wake up.
Remember.
Time to live.

What is beautiful and what is ugly?
Just like the butterfly,
the spider also deserves to be loved.

We always see only our butterflies and
the spiders we crush or lock away.

But in the end,
everything wants to be allowed to simply
be and follow its task.

To teach you what it means to be alive.

Let the butterflies fly
and the spiders run
and you will see that
what we despise
will show us that appearances are
misleading and that perhaps
spiders can teach you more
than butterflies at this time.

Your feelings want to flow like
waves without being held down.
They want to be heard,
they want to be felt
and they want to give *their message*
to you, that's the only reason
why you feel them.

Your heart is full of light
and also full of shadow.
The perfect symphony for your life.

Nothing has to become stronger
than the other, nothing has to go,
it may stay like this.

To learn what it means
to be really human here *on this earth*.

Even if you have given up
believing in it.
There is a power within you
that no one can see
and that is why it doesn't seem
to be there.
But it is there and
it always will be.

Do not lose hope in it.
You will recognize it
when you need it the most.

At some time you will realize
that the greatest pain you feel,
will be your *biggest teacher* in life.

Maybe you are ashamed
of the scars you carry.
Maybe you think you have to hide
your inner brokenness.
Maybe you think that you're not allowed
to be vulnerable.
Maybe you think you have to wear an
armor to protect yourself.
Maybe you think you have to wear a mask
because you have to hide the real you
from others.

All of that just makes you human
and it's time to let go
of all the pressure for perfection
and *just be human* again.

Life is often challenging, but that
doesn't make it any less worth living.

Embrace it.

Live through the challenge and you will
realize that you were born,
to *grow* through it.

You may think...
That your gentleness has no place.
That your scars are too ugly.
That your vulnerability makes you weak.
Your otherness means
you are not welcome.
Your kindness is too naive.
Your big dreams are too unrealistic.
Your love is too much,
but all of that
is what makes you so beautiful.

We all have it in us,
it just seems like you're the only one.
We all hide it
because we've been told not to be that.

But what you want to be and
what you don't want to be
is up to you.

Hide no longer what you really are.
Stand up and share your uniqueness
with the world.

You don't have to overcome your fear.
You don't have to fight your fear.

All it wants
is *to be loved*.

Why do you resist
being yourself so much
when you can't change who you are?

Darling, you can't change who you are,
but you *can change how you see yourself.*

You can learn
to find your way home again.

In a world that constantly
says "no" to you,
be rebellious enough
to say *YES to yourself.*

A "no" from others doesn't mean
you have to say "no" to yourself.

Just because people
have made you feel wrong
doesn't mean you are wrong.

You may be wrong for others,
but please *don't be wrong for yourself.*

Never ask yourself if your heart
is too weak to feel the pain.

Your heart is the strongest part of you.
It is already covered with scars
and has survived all the wounds.

That is why it is able
to *overcome* this pain again.

Your dream exists within you
because it was given to you.
Because life believes
that you can realize it.
Because it exists in you,
it is already real.

Just because others
don't believe in your dream
doesn't mean it can't become real.

People don't believe in your dream
because they gave up theirs long ago.

Be brave enough *to believe in something*,
to see something before it is there.

Go ahead and give people around you
permission to believe
in something too.

Everyone wants to be
the best version of themselves.
But no one wants to be
what they are right now.

In every moment you say to yourself,
"I need to be that", you say,
"What I am right now is not enough".

Never forget:
Don't only see what you're not,
see all the things you already are.
You are enough, right now.

You don't need any proof of that.
NEVER.

You are the *medicine* this world needs.

Forgiveness:
We all want to be free,
but we have a hard time letting go
of our guilt.
Honestly, it is an illusion to think
that you will be truly free
if you hold on to the feeling of guilt.

To forgive does not mean
to prove the other person right
or to give them the power,
it means to give yourself freedom.
It does not mean accepting the situation
or thinking it is good.

It means to accept that it happened and
that you cannot change it anymore.
It means to let it be as it is
and to realize that you can now decide
what kind of person this has made of you.

Forgiveness is like releasing *a caged bird*.
To admit to yourself
that you have not lost your wings
and you deserve to fly again.

You have learned
how to be kind to others,
but no one has told you
how to be kind to yourself.

So be your teacher
in the endless ocean of judgment
and guide your way back home
to a safe place ruled by kindness.

Self-love may be a lifelong journey,
but self-acceptance begins
with one decision.

You can hold on
to the hate on the outside
or be brave enough to find
your way back to yourself,
regardless of what you are
pleases others.

Sometimes it feels
like the storm will be there endlessly

never forget that just as it comes,
so it will go

because life strives for balance
so keep moving on

give yourself into the flow of life,
take its hand and it will show
you the way back home.

Sometimes it's overwhelming
to know that you can be anything,
maybe it even scares you.

But at the same time,
the greatest act of freedom
is to become aware that you are
absolutely free in your possibilities.

Yes, maybe it scares you and
yet it *is the truth*.

There may be a war within you,
you speak the language of self-judgment,
the painful words of hate,
but just as you have learned
to speak this language,
you can also put down your weapons and
learn a new one.

It is simply training,
old things must be unlearned
and new words must be understood.

You can learn the *language of self-love*.
It just takes a little time.

In all those struggles,
don't forget to *take yourself by the hand*
and keep moving forward.

you're never alone

Sometimes I go through the day and feel the pain of the whole world inside of me.

Every time you feel and heal
a piece of pain inside you,
you heal a little bit
of the pain in the world.

Remember, *pain is not meaningless.*

Pain is not against you.
Pain is always *what you make out of it.*

It's okay to fall back on *old stories*
but never forget,
only because it feels familiar
doesn't mean that it will bring you
the peace you're searching for.

There will always be moments in life
when you want to give up,
there will always be moments
when you have to ask yourself:
"Do I give up or do I go on"?
and every time you get up again
and go on,
you will trust yourself a bit more
and realize that you were
born to get up again.

It's about stopping to find reasons
why I am wrong
and trying every day
to accept my flaws.

Learn to say yes after every no
and know that no's on the outside
weigh less, more and more

because the *yes to myself*
will become stronger
than ever before.

There is someone shouting at you.

The *little child* in you
wants to feel seen and wants your love,
so it's your moment
to give this child the love
it never received.

I put my heart in a cage
because I thought that would create security

but what I didn't know was
that every day
my heart felt these boundaries,
it didn't get the nourishment
my heart was born for.

Yeah, it was always love
and without love giving or receiving
the heart wilted like a flower without water.

We think heart walls are our safe place
but it's only an illusion
because our heart doesn't want to be secure
it wants to be free and love wild,
like the wind raging above the sea.

Laugh about
the *clumsy human being* you are.
You don't know how this life should work.
But you get up every morning
and are brave enough to step out
into this world.

It doesn't matter
how much pain you feel in the moment,
your *life will go on*.

There will come a moment
when you realize,
why this pain is important for you
and what you have learned from it.

A *regression* does not mean
that you have lost something,
but that life is testing you again
to see if you have understood
what you have learned before.

There is a reason
you are the person you are.
I know sometimes
you want to be anything other than
yourself, but you are here
because you are *supposed to be* here.
It doesn't matter
if others understand you,
know for yourself
that you don't need to be
understood by others
just to be able to live here.

You exist here
because *life believes in you.*

Every thought
is a seed of hate or love,
choose wisely.

One day these *seeds will bloom*.

Your *pain guides you home.*
You can always choose to find healing
because to heal is a decision you make.

You don't need to wait
until someone says that you are enough.

You were, are, and
ever will be *enough*.

You were born enough
and you will never ever lose that.

Look into the mirror,
look into your eyes,
deeper
and without judging yourself.

What do you see?
"Oh, *I see myself*".

You don't have to be anybody
to be somebody.

In your consciousness
lies the key to *becoming free.*

People think about you
what they think about themselves.

The way others treat you,
they treat themselves.

People project their thoughts about
themselves onto you.

So never forget:
No matter how others treat you,
it has nothing to do with you
but with them.

It is their pain.
It is their thoughts.
Not yours.

Maybe time will bring you
the healing you desire - be patient.
We don't always have to fix everything,
sometimes it fixes itself.

Let it be,
be with it
and *it will heal*, you will see.

No human has the right to decide
if you are beautiful or not.

You are *beauty itself*.
Reclaim your beauty.

You don't need to do anything,
to be beautiful,
okay?

You can't lose the ability to love,
because you are *love itself*.

Every human that hurt me
taught me *a lesson about kindness.*

We do not heal by staying in our light
but by diving
into *our own darkness.*

I give up having to be enough
in this world
because I have finally understood
that I will never be enough
if I give everything that I have
to become enough.

This life is about remembering
that every single one of us
is already enough
and we don't have to earn
our right to be who we are.

How can I live my best life
if people suffer at the same time?

"Yeah, but nothing changes
if you suffer with them".

So be the change.

We don't want pain
but we hold it in our hearts
because being in our pain
gives us meaning
in a very strange way

hold our *hearts closed*
because we think this is safe

trying to heal
but in the end, we don't want
that our wounds become scars

hold on to old stories
because they are what we know

and give everything to stay
in our little cage
we once built because we are too afraid
to keep moving on

out into the great world
and learn what life is really about.

Tear down
all the walls around your heart
and allow your love to flow again.
Show your scars,
they don't make you vulnerable,
you can wear them with pride.

They make you a human being,
that *loves honestly*.

People told me that I'm too much.
I've thought a lot about letting go
of the love I give, my joy, my passion and
my inner fire.

Until the day I realized, if I would let go
of that, I would lose myself.

Never be someone else
just because some humans told you,
that you're not enough
for just being yourself.

Do not hold back
the storm in you
any moment longer,
let it rage
and set you free.

People are jealous of you
if they want to be like you.

Jealousy is the *key to inspiration.*

It is not your task
to become something special
but to live the special *you already are.*

Your value does not depend on
whether others like you or not.

It is not your job
to be good enough for others.

You are *good enough*
and you don't need to earn proof of it.

You are changing
the whole world right now
because you are here.

Everything influences everything.
Everything is connected
to each other.

Stop thinking that you don't make
a difference in this world,
you can change everything.

And who knows, maybe your smile
will save someone else's day.

Don't *walk away form your path*.
Only because someone
lets you doubt about your way.

We are all afraid
to lose the people we love.
There is no medicine for loss
except the belief
that we will see them again someday.

That maybe they will never be gone,
and we will always be able to feel them.

One thing I know for sure is,
that it is braver to love than not to love
out of fear of the pain that may come
when the person leaves.

Maybe this is how life teaches us
to take the risk to love now
and not to wait.

You don't have to function to be lovable.
Mistakes don't define who you are.

They only show you *your humanity*.

What hurts is not the rejection
on the outside,
but how much I *lost myself*
on the way to give everything
to please this person.

The path to inner peace begins with
saying YES to yourself.

Yes to your mistakes,
yes to your past,
yes to everything that makes you YOU,
yes to everything that bothers you
about yourself, it belongs to you.

As long as you fight against who you are,
you will always be dissatisfied.

The ability to accept what is
gives you the *freedom to change* it.

If you want to live,
live in the present moment.

Not your past and not your future,
in the time you think about
the present moment, and think about
why it isn't like you want it,
the moment is already gone.

Time flows,
but do you flow with your life?

We learned that we need to strive for
perfection instead of living the process

No mistakes allowed,
you don't have time to learn,
no, when it takes too long, give it up,
you will find something better,
they told us.

But life is all about learning
and falling in love with the process,
with the ups and downs
and looking at some day back in the past
and be so proud of yourself
because you've learned something new
and *grow higher than ever before*.

Forgiveness is giving yourself
the freedom you deserve.
You do not forgive for others,
you *forgive for yourself.*

With every heartbeat, your heart
whispers to you
"I am here, I am love, I am enough".

Listen to your heart.
It sets *the direction for your life.*

It's absolutely understandable to become
hard and emotionally untouchable

because in a world like this
where kind hearts are so rare
it's easier to close all of yourself down
than to keep all of your power
and let your heart stay open

but please from my heart to yours

I know you're hurt

I know there are so many wounds

but don't hurt yourself
only because you thought
that what you are is not enough

try every day to open your heart
a little bit more
and then you realize
that we only hurt each other
because everyone is hurt

someone needs to say stop
and maybe it's you - I *hope so*

I know you are tempted to carry on
the pain others have caused you,
it's okay to feel that way.

But in the end,
you don't have the permission
to treat others like shit
just because you've been treated
like shit.

Let yourself be at peace and
break the cycle of suffering.

I know it's not easy, but it doesn't make
you free to inflict pain on others
even if you think it does.

It is easy to walk the path of guilt
but it is truly brave
to walk the path of healing.

You are the change the world needs.
I am proud of you and yes I see you.
Someday the world will thank you
because we all need people like you,
YOU are the hero the world needs.
Yes, exactly you.

Don't forget
you don't have to be free of pain
to be able to be loved by others.

You don't need to be perfect, for love.

Please understand
that you do not have to hide or protect
yourself from life.

Your life is there
to let you be *touched by it*.

Life doesn't come to you,
you are the one who creates life.

Suppressing your power
just to avoid attention
may hurt more at some point
than taking the risk
of showing yourself
in your rawest and most genuine form.

Yes, maybe you will be judged for it,
but *you will anyway*,
it doesn't matter
if you stay where you are
or expose who you truly are
to the world.

4

CHAPTER

awakening

This moment is all that counts
right now,
your past doesn't define your future
and your future is on the way.
Stay in the present moment
and you will lose yourself in *eternity*.

my mind wants to understand
my heart wants *just to be*

Whatever needs to be, it may be.
There is a *place for everything*
inside of me.

People don't have to understand you,
maybe they never will, it's okay.

It's just that you know
for yourself *who you are*,
that's enough.

Why do women and men fight each other,
why does one gender have to be better
than the other?

Why can't we just complement
each other in our *opposites*
and celebrate each other
in our *equalities?*

No one else can tell you
if your life is *worth living* or not.

Only YOU can do that.

Humanity has become strange to us.
Because we have been too busy
minimizing our weaknesses,
hiding our vulnerabilities,
and judging each other for our flaws.

We had to become perfect,
to play the perfect role in order to lose
the affection of others.

Do we want to live in a world where
authenticity has become a rarity,
just because there is no place for simply
being human anymore?

Being a human doesn't make us weak
No, it makes us *incredibly strong*.

Even if you feel empty within yourself,
I see so much that does not
make you empty.
So much beauty,
potential,
value,
love and kindness
waiting to be seen by yourself.

Open your eyes and really look,
it is all there, ready to be found.

Perhaps the "perfect"
lies in the *imperfect*

being human in a world full of perfection
is the *biggest risk* we can take
and at the same time
the most *selfless thing* we can do.

The more we look for something
and want to force something,
the more life says:
"Learn to let go and then we'll talk again".

Life has its own plan for you
and it always wants the best,
trust that everything will come
at the right time.

You will never lose your beauty.
Maybe you've just forgotten
what it feels like to feel beautiful.

People are like stars.
Each so unique, but *yet all the same*.

They shine together.
Always.

Perhaps we find the greatest treasures
in the *places we fear the most.*

People will say to you,
how you should be and what you can't be,
but is that the truth or only *their reality*?

Some people will be by your side
your whole journey of life.
Others will leave you. This fact hurts.

But who says that impermanence doesn't
just want to teach us to love now
and not wait for later?

Yes, sometimes love hurts,
but doesn't it hurt more
to never have loved?

Love is what will always remain with you.
Because you are made of love.
Love is you. *So go your way in love.*

Everyone talks about pollution
but nobody talks about the pollution of
your inner world

*What if the state of the world reflects only
the inner world of us?*

Maybe it wasn't a failure,
maybe it was *the best* thing
that could have happened to you.

(at some point you will understand
that, trust me)

A bird that has been caged all its life
forgets that it can fly.

But that doesn't mean,
that its *wings are broken*.

People have told you what you're
allowed
to be and what not.

Be rebellious enough to live and
celebrate the parts
that you were rejected for
on the outside.

They make you
the great and unique person you are.

Stop being told
what you can and can't be.
Free yourself from external validation.
Be the person you are.

Don't allow yourself to reject
something in you
just because it is too different
for this world,
just because it seems to be too much.

Because it is rejected, it is needed.
This world needs your uniqueness.
This world needs you,
as *a sign that everything has its place*.

You do not have to be perfect
to call yourself spiritual.

Spirituality doesn't mean
being guided by rules
it's about letting go
of who you need to be
and remembering *that you be it all.*

It's not about being perfect,
it's about living,
it's about being real.

This world doesn't need perfect people,
it needs *real humans*.

It's not about striving
to never be sad again,
never be angry again,
never feel pain or fear again.

It's about welcoming every feeling and
learning to *give everything a place*.

Sadness teaches you that you can love.

Anger teaches you that you are a person
who wants to be heard and seen.

Pain teaches you that you are vulnerable
and that it's okay.

Fear teaches you
that you have an incredible amount
of courage inside of you.

They are not negative feelings,
they are feelings that have been made
into something bad, yet they have just
as much value as feelings we like more.

Your existence proves
that you *deserve to be loved*.

It will always be so.
You don't have to do anything
to prove that.

Ups and downs in the adventure of life:

days when you...
feel beautiful
and days when absolutely not.

feel satisfied and days when you are
absolutely dissatisfied.

like people and others on which you just
want to be by yourself because others
overwhelm you.

believe in yourself and others when you
doubt yourself

go through the world with an open heart
and others where you hide it.

when you love life and others
when you are lying on the ground and you
have to use all your strength to get up
again.

you think you know yourself and others
were it feels like you have lost yourself

It's okay.
Every phase of life deserves to be lived.

Like every human being
you do *your best* here in this life,
you may not understand
the actions of others
and yet they try just like you
to survive
and provide for their well-being.

It is not what is,
it is *your story* that you tell yourself
about what is.

For me, spirituality means
connecting the human form with my soul

my eye of a human will always cry
when it looks at the world
but my soul's eye
will always know that
everything *will be fine*.

What success means to others
doesn't have to be
your image of success.

Never strive for something
you don't really want
with all your heart.

No one has to *understand your path*.

You don't have to do anything
to be valuable.

The moment that I set myself free,
was the moment I realized that *my worth*
isn't dependent if you love me or not.

As a soul in this human form,
I don't need to decide to be one thing.

No, the idea of this life
is *being anything*.

One day I realized
that the quiet voice
my younger self heard
at the lowest moments,
was the future self of mine
spoke with softness and wisdom
to *keep her alive.*

I hope that someday
you will realize
that you don't need
to hide your love from the world
because all the world needs
is you and *all the love you hide.*

We strive for happiness in the future
without understanding
that happiness
can *only be felt in the present moment.*

You never learned to be kind to yourself
so never forget
that one part of you learned
that you need to hate yourself
to stay alive.

It's a hard illusion you hold on to
but we all do it.

Please use every day to learn kindness
like you learned to be kind to others.

Yeah, you will fail often
that's life.

All you can do is show yourself
a kind heart and keep moving on.

*Be your cheerleader in tough times and
the hero that saves you in the endless nights.*

Maybe deep down you believe
that there is no place for you
in this world.

Please understand:
You are here for a reason,
your birth was the sign
that you have a place
here in this world.

You are welcome, just as you are.
You were born to be YOURSELF.

Every day you can decide
if you exist in the dream of the ego
or if you live
in the *clear sky of reality*

You don't live this life
to force you into something
you've never wanted.

Never forget your permission from life
to *create your own magical path*.

It is not only about learning
to believe in your abilities
but above all
to *believe in who you are.*

I know you fight every day
ask yourself:
Is it *for you*
or against you?

It's not about the fear of disappointment.
It's about what you do with
disappointment.

It's about how much *power* you give
external circumstances over you.

I know there exists
a lot of pressure in you,
in every moment
you need to make a decision.

You think, it's forever
and you can't change
what you have decided.
That's not the truth, my love.

In every moment you can *choose again*,
make a new decision
or change your opinion.

Life
does not have to be understood
in order *to be lived*

People
do not need to be understood
in order *to be loved*

World peace does
not begin on the outside.
It begins within you.

Some people will leave.
But you will always stay.

Because you will
always *be your home*

Something is calling you
and you cannot deny it.

You are here for a reason,
there is something for you
to do here.

You will find your way again and again
to what you are supposed to do,
until you dare to take the step
to follow the call.

Don't be afraid of your *calling*,
you are ready
or you wouldn't be able to hear it.

You came here because you are ready.
You were born to show us all,
what your destiny in this life is about.

We all search for the great meaning
in life:

What if the meaning is life itself?
What if you are the meaning?

We search outside and forget that
everything we need
can be found within ourselves,
we have simply forgotten it.

We all feel that pressure and desire
to always *be happy*.

But maybe that's not the point:
Maybe we find true happiness when we
are simply at peace with what is.
When we stop wanting to be
something and just be.
When we stop judging certain parts
and just accept what is.

Healing may take time.
But healing also begins
with a clear decision.

The path to healing
will take a lot of strength,
and at some point
the time will come
to let go of the past.

It is like river water.
If you swirl around in it with your hands,
the dirt will rise to the bottom;
if it is allowed to rest,
everything will find its place.

So healing is a journey
and at the same time letting it rest.
Life strives for healing,
so don't be afraid of not being able
to overcome your past someday.

Life is with you every step of the way.
But the decision to let go
will have to come from yourself.

You will always be judged
for what you are.

No matter how successful,
"perfect", beautiful or adjusted
you try to be.

People always judge.
What this means is
that it should not be about the claim
to no longer be judged
but simply to be you and to gain
distance from the judgments
on the outside.

Judgments say nothing about you
only *about the other person*.

One day you will realize
that all the stories
you have told about yourself,
why you can't do things,
why you're not enough and
will always stay in pain,
are just stories that also can be fairytales
instead of the truth about yourself.

Always ask yourself:
is this the reality or only a story?
and choose wisely in connection
with the part in you
that knows exactly who you really are.

That's what I call *awakening*.

The goal of *perfection is an illusion* created to limit you in your existence.

We think our destiny is to live a life
that is determined by others.
We think we can't change anything
and that we are helplessly lost
at the mercy of others.

This is not the truth and deep inside
you know it.

It is your life and you decide
what you will do with it.

Sometimes we fall down into ashes,
but there will come a time when we
burn brighter than ever before.

Without this process,
we wouldn't be able
to let go
of our old identities.

Fall in love with the ups and downs.
Fall in love with the process.
Fall in love with your human experience.
Fall in love with moments of tears and
moments of pure happiness.

Honey that's life.

You can either live
or stay in your head
and wait for perfection.

I walked away from my home
because I thought it would make
me free, but now I know,
I can only become free
from the inside not from the outside,
because *everything starts in myself.*

Sometimes everything becomes dark,
don't forget that darkness is not bad,
you choose what darkness is
and *what it will become.*

.

We all want to be something,
but maybe we just never find peace in
having to be something,
but in letting go of everything you
thought you had to live up to.

Maybe it's just about being you.

Maybe there will come the day
when you realize who you really are
and forget who you think
you should be...

We lose ourselves in probabilities
instead of seeing our possibilities

Don't give other people
the permission to define who you are.

What we need
will always find us.

I am...

It's your decision.

Go one step and then another
until you get it.
Every step counts, so start walking.
It's not about wanting to walk,
it's about taking the first step.

You can stay in the dust
or you go in one direction
and find *a way out of it*.

You aren't the victim of your life.
You are the holy creator.

Every thought, every feeling and
everything you do is your choice.

If you always choose safety,
a part of you will wilt.

Because you were born to live
brave and honest.

Safety is an illusion,
you think you are safe but you aren't.

Life is in constant change,
so go with life, and live truly.

I know this hurts, but it will also
make you *unbelievably free*.

We fear death.
but we are more afraid of LIFE.

You don't need to do something
to be loved.
You don't need to find proof
that you deserve love.
Your existence is the proof.

The freedom you seek, my love,
is to be found where everything
is as it is, in the present moment.

Find the *present moment*
and you will be free.

You don't need
recognition from others,
to feel seen.

Maybe your inner fire
doesn't always ignite from love, maybe
sometimes also
from *deep pain*.

There will be angels in your life
and people who bring you learning.
Be grateful *for every one*.

We are not disconnected.
Everyone feels her-/himself different
and with this thought we feel alone.

The truth is,
*we are all the same
and we are all one.*

Maybe I don't fit into this world.
But maybe this world
doesn't fit me either.

You may think that you are not welcome
in this world.

But that is not the truth.
You *just don't feel welcome.*

You are a dreamer?
How brave that you keep dreaming...

But don't let your dreams
stay pictures in your mind,
dreams are here to be lived.

There is a reason
why this dream exists in you,
so *don't ignore it*.

The greatest fear we humans have
is the fear of being ourselves.
No one can take away the fear
of being judged,
but you can give yourself the permission
to live in the unknown
and give yourself the understanding
you seek.

We think our intuition
needs to give us answers right now,
but maybe it's a process,
of feeling into the different possibilities
and letting grow the truth like a little
seed in your heart.

Intuition is not always the easy way to
take
it's often the hard one,
the one that lets you go into the dark cave.

Yes, we all are afraid,
of changing our ways
and taking our chances to become.
But do you want to stay at the same point
for your whole life
or get all your courage together
and say yes to the possibility
to growing?

In the end it's all about
growing into the wonderful flower
you're destined to be
since you were planted into this world.

Life and its intentions:

It triggers your fears
until you say yes to go through it

It always wants to remind
you about your potential

It wants to flow and be the playground
of your journey of becoming

You need to learn to surrender
and let go of your beliefs
about how life should be

It's your greatest lover
and best friend at once,
because it will always
want the best and give you everything
you need until you find your way
back home.

Every person here on this earth craves
love.
This fact doesn't make us weak,
it unites us.

This thing we call life:

And sometimes we're just feeling lost
in this thing we call life
not knowing if we should
go forward or go back,
if we should go right or left.

What we feel is just too much and
our thoughts are drowning us,
stealing the air in our lungs
the anxiety and panic that hold us back
in the prison we once built.

But the truth is
that prison isn't what life is about
it's just what others teach us
what life should be.

We are free that's the truth
and living life is just unwinding
all the illusions that once felt right.

Maybe it's just about standing still
and starting to listen to yourself
because there is
the truth yet to be found.

Fall to the deepest grounds of oceans
learn to swim in your emotions.
Open your heart after deeply shaken
losses.
Rise up like a phoenix
from the fire that burnt old stories
about your own limits and doubts.
feel moments of pure bliss,
make adventures
in the magical beauty we call earth.
Find out what love feels like,
learn about *the journey*
of being a human.

That's what I call being alive.

You will always see
what *your mind* wants to see

I always searched
for meaning in the world,
but one day I realized
that I will never find anyone
who can tell me where to find it.

I realized that I will find it,
in *the meaning I give to the world*

Thank you

I thought I need to find
the formula for living life.
But instead I found
the simplest but most healing secret.
Thank you they whispered. Thank you.
Two words as strong as nothing else.
They bring light into the darkest moments,
because they let me surrender.
The monsters become angels, teachers and
gatekeepers from hell back to heaven.
They let me feel life again.
All the love that exists.
They let me become one
with the beauty and magic around me
and just teach me,
that life is always giving me the best.

Maybe I will not understand it now,
but thank you
for teaching me what life is about.
It's about the fallings and the setbacks,
it's about the pain and the love,
it's about the chances that let us heal,
about the jumps into the unknown
that maybe started with feeling wrong,
but teach us
that change needs time to let us see
what we become.*

*Thank you - let us plant the seed
of living life so truly.
It gives us peace and makes us free,
of suffering in the drama
we thought we were
and finding our way back to the truth.

So give up your resistance
and let life in again.
Bathe in life, soak in the wonders
and open your heart with every thank you
a little bit more.

Thank you it's what you are
and what you will become.
It's purpose and it's soul.
It's the truth that brings us home.

Why do people live here
when everything is so painful?

Because deep down they know that life
is *so much more than pain*.

Boundaries are important.
But I don't want to hide myself
behind walls
and not be touched by other people
and life anymore.
I don't want to be untouchable and cold.
No, *I want to live and feel.*

I hope you will realize
that you don't need a hero
that saves you
in the darkest nights.

No.
You will remember
that the hero
who always saved you
was yourself.

Be proud of yourself, little life-hero.

The gap of eternity:
And on some days we aren't sure
about life or ourselves.
But that doesn't mean
that our purpose isn't being alive,
because it is and always will be,
it's just about remembering
the dance between darkness and light
and the gap of eternity in between.

Since the moment I was born,
I became *the hummingbird*
that is nourished by the nectar of life

My love

We are at the end of this book
and I hope it helps you to find
some steps closer back home to yourself,
because you deserve nothing else than that.

Know that you're enough, by being yourself.
Stop fighting against yourself
and allow yourself to go your own unique path.

I send you endless love on your way of life.
A big hug and never forget:
This world is so much more beautiful,
with you as a part of it.

I see you, thank you that you are here

with love
Isabella Maria

Thanks for giving me your time,
what a gift and I hope
you find so much inspiration
and that you feel a little bit more okay
about who you are.
*Because being you is your destiny
and a gift for us all.*

THANK YOU WITH ALL MY HEART.

About the author:

Isabella Maria Rösli is a young
woman from Switzerland.

Since she was a kid she never felt
herself welcome on this earth.
It took a long time for her to find
her place and to find peace with
living this life.

She wants to remind people about
their uniqueness, their humanity,
their potential, their beauty and
give them the feeling of being
understood.

Isabella, believes in kindness, love
and that we all just give our best
to find out, what this life
is truly about.

Isabella would love to connect with you:
https://www.puresoul-coaching.com